Taylor Swift

By Holly C. Corbett, Beatrice Forman,
Ben Jhoty, Maura K. Johnston, Scott Raab,
Carissa Rosenberg Tozzi & Annie Zaleski

HEARST
HOME

Contents

7 TAYLOR NOW

38 TEEN YEARS

71 TWENTIES

107 THIRTIES

Taylor wears an Atelier Versace bodysuit during the Eras tour in Paris, May 2024.

Taylor

NOW

WHY TAYLOR, WHY NOW?

In 1984, there was no bigger pop star than Michael Jackson. Hot off *Thriller*, the highest-selling album of all time, Jackson was possibly the most famous man alive. From São Paulo to Saint Petersburg, if you asked any person on the street who he was, they would know.

Previously, only The Beatles and Elvis Presley had reached such heights.

Taylor Swift, at 34, currently boasts levels of fame, power, and influence that even surpass Jackson's. Named *TIME*'s 2023 Person of the Year, Taylor's Eras Tour was the first to generate over $1 billion in revenue. And its cinematic release was the highest-grossing concert film in history, earning $261.6 million in global box office sales, knocking off Jackson's *This Is It*.

Taylor's achievements in the recording industry are astonishing enough, but her popularity and ensuing influence have now spilled into other domains.

Her romance with Kansas City Chiefs tight end Travis Kelce united sports and pop-culture fans and created a boon for the NFL. Her game attendance boosted average viewership to 17.9 million people, a 7 percent increase from 2022, according to Nielsen.

Taylor's influence doesn't end there. She has transformed the fortunes of fashion brands, often creating instant sellouts when she supports a brand. She has led style trends with her elevated mix of girl-next-door and comfort chic and has prompted a surge in friendship bracelets.

All this has had an almost immediate commercial impact: The *Washington Post* estimated that the Eras Tour would generate a $5.7 billion bump in consumer spending in North America alone.

Clearly Taylor wields an unprecedented sovereign-state level of soft-power influence. But if you really want to get an idea of how big Taylor is, look to politics. In 2023 she encouraged her 272 million Instagram followers to raise their

Taylor performing on May 12, 2024 in an Alberta Ferretti gown during the *folklore* and *evermore* set on the fourth night of her sold-out Eras run in Paris.

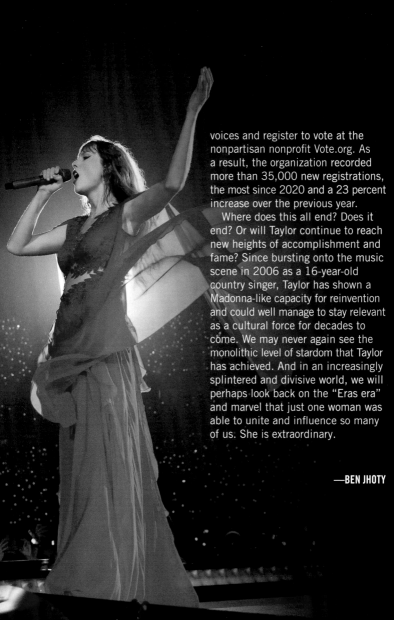

voices and register to vote at the nonpartisan nonprofit Vote.org. As a result, the organization recorded more than 35,000 new registrations, the most since 2020 and a 23 percent increase over the previous year.

Where does this all end? Does it end? Or will Taylor continue to reach new heights of accomplishment and fame? Since bursting onto the music scene in 2006 as a 16-year-old country singer, Taylor has shown a Madonna-like capacity for reinvention and could well manage to stay relevant as a cultural force for decades to come. We may never again see the monolithic level of stardom that Taylor has achieved. And in an increasingly splintered and divisive world, we will perhaps look back on the "Eras era" and marvel that just one woman was able to unite and influence so many of us. She is extraordinary.

—BEN JHOTY

TAYLOR SWIFT

BY THE NUMBERS

"I love numbers. Numbers rule my world," Taylor Swift told Paul McCartney in a "Musicians on Musicians" interview in *Rolling Stone*. Just look at the way she's made 13 her lucky number. "I was born on the 13th," she told *MTV News* in 2009. "I turned 13 on Friday the 13th. My first album went gold in 13 weeks. My first number one song had a 13-second intro ["Our Song," which reached the top of **Billboard's** Hot Country Songs in 2007]." Taylor used to write the number on her hand before every show and continues to incorporate 13 into everything from release dates to video Easter eggs to track lists.

Taylor has made other numbers significant in her career while racking up impressive achievements on the charts, on the road, and at award shows. Here are 13 numbers that illuminate key moments in Taylor's life and career.

Taylor paints her lucky number 13 on her hand before the 2009 Madison Square Garden stop on the Speak Now tour. A pre-performance ritual from earlier in her career, Taylor nods to it in the music video for "I Can See You," a vault track on *Speak Now (Taylor's Version)*.

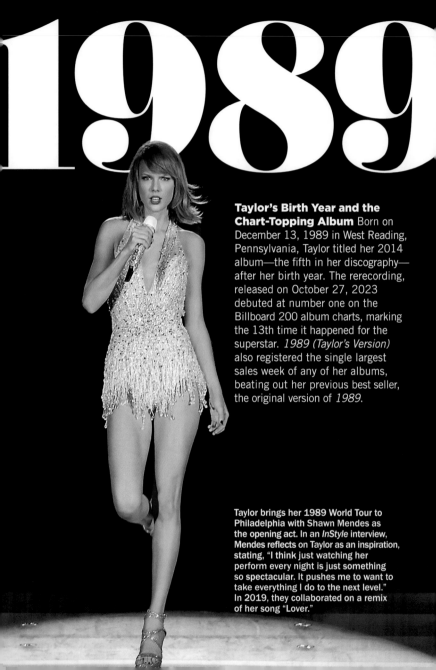

1989

Taylor's Birth Year and the Chart-Topping Album Born on December 13, 1989 in West Reading, Pennsylvania, Taylor titled her 2014 album—the fifth in her discography—after her birth year. The rerecording, released on October 27, 2023 debuted at number one on the Billboard 200 album charts, marking the 13th time it happened for the superstar. *1989 (Taylor's Version)* also registered the single largest sales week of any of her albums, beating out her previous best seller, the original version of *1989*.

Taylor brings her 1989 World Tour to Philadelphia with Shawn Mendes as the opening act. In an *InStyle* interview, Mendes reflects on Taylor as an inspiration, stating, "I think just watching her perform every night is just something so spectacular. It pushes me to want to take everything I do to the next level." In 2019, they collaborated on a remix of her song "Lover."

Singing at a 76ers Game Helped Launch Her Career

In the spring of 2002, the then-12-year-old Taylor sang "The Star-Spangled Banner" before the NBA's Philadelphia 76ers tipped off against the Detroit Pistons. A former babysitter of Taylor's who worked for the Sixers brokered the deal. Taylor also performed the national anthem at hundreds of sporting events, including before Game 3 of the 2008 World Series in Philadelphia. "When I was 11 years old, it occurred to me that the national anthem was the best way to get in front of a large group of people if you don't have a record deal," she told *Rolling Stone* in 2008. "So I started singing the national anthem anywhere I possibly could…I've sung that song many, many, many times and it still gives me chills."

The Age Taylor Broke Her First Record At 14, she became the youngest songwriter to be signed to the publishing company Sony/ATV. "Most people find out what they're going to be when they're in college," Taylor said in 2005, when Nashville station WSMV profiled the way she was balancing high school and her music career—her first TV interview. "But I guess for me it just came a little earlier."

20

The Youngest Winner of Album of the Year Taylor turned 20 the month before her second album, *Fearless*, won Album of the Year at the 52nd Annual Grammy Awards in 2010. This win made her the youngest person to nab that trophy. She'd relinquish that record in 2020, when 18-year-old Billie Eilish won the award.

14

Taylor backstage at the 2010 Grammy Awards with Liz Rose, who cowrote the singles "White Horse" and "You Belong with Me" on *Fearless*.

Taylor performs at the Red Tour stop in Denver on June 2, 2013.

Damages Taylor Received From a DJ

In 2015, Denver DJ David Mueller filed a defamation suit after Taylor publicly alleged that the radio host had groped her in 2013. Taylor countersued, asking for damages of one dollar because she didn't want to bankrupt the radio host—she wanted only to send a public message: "It means 'no means no' and it tells every woman they will decide what will be tolerated with their body," Taylor's attorney, Douglas Baldridge, said in his closing remarks to a Denver jury, who ruled in Taylor's favor.

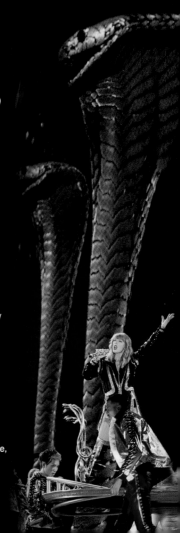

63'

Length of the Clapback Snake on the Reputation Tour Karyn is the name of the 63-foot inflatable cobra who popped up onstage during Taylor's 2018 Reputation Stadium Tour. Inspired by Kim Kardashian calling Taylor a snake during the drawn-out public feud with her then-husband Kanye West, Karyn not only became an eye-popping sight during the high-energy Reputation shows, it brought Taylor a bit of joy: "I can't tell you how hard I had to keep from laughing every time my 63-foot inflatable cobra named Karyn appeared onstage in front of 60,000 screaming fans," she wrote in an essay for *Elle* in 2019.

Karyn looms fiercely above Taylor and dancers during the 2018 Reputation Stadium Tour in Glendale, Arizona. Taylor later described the stage prop snake as "the stadium tour equivalent of responding to a troll's hateful Instagram comment with 'lol.'"

31

Total Award-Winning Tracks Released in 2020 During the COVID-19 lockdown, Taylor wrote and recorded *folklore* and *evermore*, two folky, homespun albums that represented a new approach to her storytelling. "I found myself not only writing my own stories but also writing about or from the perspective of people I've never met, people I've known, or those I wish I hadn't," she wrote in the introduction to *folklore*. A hidden message lurked within those releases: "There are 16 tracks on *folklore*; there are 15 tracks on *evermore*. Add 'em up," she told Jimmy Kimmel in December 2020. "What do you get? In my mind, it's just the opposite. It's just 13 backward." The two releases earned Taylor a Guinness World Record for the shortest gap between new number one albums on the U.S. **Billboard** 200 for a female artist, and both albums were nominated for the Grammys' Album of the Year, which *folklore* won.

Taylor, seen here as she performs the *folklore* portion of her Eras Tour in November 2023. "My world felt opened up creatively," she told Apple Music about the way the album has changed her approach to songwriting. "There was a point that I got to as a writer who only wrote very diaristic songs that I felt it was unsustainable for my future moving forward. So what I felt after we put out *folklore* was like, 'Oh wow, people are into this too, this thing that feels really good for my life and feels really good for my creativity.'

The Track When Taylor's Albums Typically Crest

According to *Vulture*, Taylor's albums tend to reach their first big emotional peak on track 5, when "she really, fully gets cathartic." The poison-pen "Dear John" from *Speak Now*, the bereft "White Horse" from *Fearless*, the portrait of a disintegrating marriage "tolerate it" from *evermore*, the stock-taking "You're on Your Own, Kid" from *Midnights,* and the sad farewell of "So Long, London" from *The Tortured Poets Department* are all positioned at track 5 on Taylor's albums—and all provide cleansing moments worthy of their own sob sessions.

Taylor and John Mayer duet on his song "Half of My Heart" at Z100's Jingle Ball in December 2009, while they were dating. Fans believe Mayer is the subject of "Dear John," the fifth track on *Speak Now*, released in 2010 after the couple broke up.

Percentage of American Adults Who Are Taylor Fans

Right before Taylor's career-spanning retrospective Eras Tour kicked off in March 2023, a Morning Consult survey said that 53 percent of U.S. adults considered themselves Taylor Swift fans—with a robust 16 percent calling themselves "avid" fans, and 44 percent of those fans willing to call themselves Swifties.

Loyal fans, including one holding an illuminated photo of Taylor's cat Meredith Grey, scream for the pop icon at the Staples Center in Los Angeles during the 1989 World Tour in August 2015.

53%

Stops on the Record-Breaking Eras Tour

At press time, the Eras Tour had 152 dates on its itinerary. The show allowed Taylor to spotlight the four albums she'd released since 2018's Reputation Stadium Tour as well as the rest of her catalog. To prepare for the physically demanding tour, Taylor told *Time* that she started training six months in advance, which included singing while running on a treadmill "fast for fast songs and a jog or a fast walk for slow songs." In each city on the tour, she often performed three back-to-back shows of 40-plus songs, with at least a day of rest in bed between cities. The Eras Tour is scheduled to end in Vancouver in December 2024.

Taylor dons a glittering red coat by designer Ashish at the opening night of the Eras Tour in Glendale, Arizona on March 17, 2023. Taylor told *Time* that in advance of the tour premiere, "We actually got to be in the stadium for almost a month running the show several times a week. So that was extremely helpful." Taylor kicked off her Reputation Tour at the same stadium five years earlier.

$93 million

Opening Weekend Box Office Receipts for the Eras Concert Film

Taylor Swift: The Eras Tour, the movie version of her stadium show, opened in theaters on October 13, 2023. The first weekend's box-office receipts came in at an astonishing $92.8 million—the biggest opening-weekend gross in history for a concert film. Taylor attended the premiere at AMC the Grove 14 in LA, along with luminaries like Beyoncé, Maren Morris, and Flavor Flav. Audience members treated the movie like one of Taylor's concerts, dressing up in Eras-appropriate outfits and belting out lyrics (Taylor did too!), which set the stage for screenings to come.

Taylor arrives at *Taylor Swift: The Eras Tour* movie premiere on October 11, 2023 in a floral Oscar de la Renta gown. A few weeks later, she announced the film's December 13 streaming release date on Instagram, telling her fans it would be a "fun way to celebrate the year we've had together"–not to mention a stunning way to celebrate her 34th birthday.

Taylor Tops Charts With 10 Singles and 10 Albums—a First!

The buoyant *Lover* track "Cruel Summer" was an instant favorite among Swifties, who embraced its catchy chorus and intense bridge. On the Eras Tour, Taylor used the track as the first bridge of the evening which led to a massive increase in streaming. In response, Taylor released a single of the track, and in October 2023, it reached number one on Billboard's Hot 100. This was a career highlight—it marked Taylor's 10th single to reach the top of the singles chart and made Taylor the first female artist to score 10 chart-topping singles on the Hot 100 plus 10 number one albums on the Billboard 200 albums chart. (Her first single to top the charts? The *Red* kiss-off "We Are Never Ever Getting Back Together," originally released in 2012.)

Taylor accepts Billboard's Artist of the Year award in May 2013, a decade before she broke the record for the most Billboard chart-topping singles and albums on October 23, 2023. In her acceptance speech, she said, "To the fans who come to the shows, who buy the albums, I just want you to know this one thing: You are the longest and best relationship I have ever had."

23

Taylor's stunning Schiaparelli Grammy gown was accented by 300 carats of diamonds and a vintage watch choker with the time set to midnight for her nominated album, *Midnights*.

"For me, the award is the work."

—TAYLOR, GRAMMY ACCEPTANCE SPEECH,
February 2, 2024

Album of the Year Grammys Taylor Has Won At the 2024 Grammy Awards, Taylor won her fourth Album of the Year award for *Midnights*, making her the winningest artist in that category. She has won 14 in total out of 52 nominations. During her acceptance speech, she brought up producer Jack Antonoff and collaborator Lana Del Rey, who she called "a legend in her prime right now." She went on to say, "I would love to tell you that this is the best moment of my life, but I feel this happy when I finish a song, or when I crack the code to a bridge that I love, or when I'm short-listing a music video, or when I'm rehearsing with my dancers or my band or getting ready to go to Tokyo to play a show." She also announced her next album, *The Tortured Poets Department*, that evening.

—MAURA K.

TAYLOR'S MUSICAL EVOLUTION

Taylor and Natalie Maines of The Chicks belt out "Goodbye Earl" during the Los Angeles stop of the 1989 World Tour. Taylor later told Billboard that The Chicks "showed an entire generation of girls that female rage can be a bonding experience between us all the very second we first heard Natalie Maines bellow, 'That Earl had to DIE.'"

In August 2015, Taylor announced a special mystery guest at the Los Angeles stop on her 1989 World Tour. "I can safely and honestly say I would not be a musician if it hadn't been for this artist," Taylor said by way of introduction. "I would not have wanted to be a country music artist. If not for this woman and her band, I would not have known that you could be quirky and fun and yourself and outspoken and brave and real." After this glowing tease, Natalie Maines of The Chicks appeared onstage— and the two ran through a barn-burning, joyous version of what Taylor called her "go-to talent show song," The Chicks' 2000 hit "Goodbye Earl."

The tune—a jaunty murder ballad that finds two best friends teaming up to kill an abusive husband and then living happily ever after without him—isn't typical talent show fare. However, it makes sense that Taylor gravitated toward "Goodbye Earl." The song's lyrics cover themes that Taylor revisits in her own songs: friendship, resilience, and moving forward after a bad relationship.

Of course, Taylor's complete catalog covers far more ground thematically. She's become the biggest musician in the world today precisely because she never stops changing and pushing herself in new directions. The heart-on-sleeve journal entries of her 2006 self-titled debut gave way to 2008's *Fearless*—a mighty pop-country album that spawned two crossover hits: the *Romeo and Juliet* update "Love Story" and the aching romantic fantasy "You Belong with Me." The even more expansive 2010 release *Speak Now* found Taylor writing every song by herself, her

first time without cowriters. Buoyed by this freedom, she dipped her toes deeper into the pop music world, courtesy of songs like "Mine," a teen-movie-worthy tale of two people who find love despite their differences ("You made a rebel of a careless man's careful daughter"), while still acknowledging the rootsy country style that first propelled her to stardom.

With the release of 2012's melodic masterpiece *Red*, Taylor officially entered the pop phase of her career. The album featured collaborations with hitmakers Max Martin and Shellback on the sassy "I Knew You Were Trouble," the celebratory "22," and her first number one pop single, the catchy earworm "We Are Never Ever Getting Back Together." From here, Taylor boldly experimented with different sounds and styles: the dreamlike synth-pop of 2014's *1989*; the defiant rock and electro sounds of 2017's brash *Reputation*; and the delicate watercolor-pop of 2019's *Lover*. These albums all sound

DISCOGRAPHY

Taylor Swift (2006)

Fearless (2008)

Speak Now (2010)

different—and they all propelled Taylor's career like a rocket.

Artists generally build their careers in one genre, attracting audiences who appreciate a specific style of music. So why did Taylor's popularity keep growing even as her music kept changing? For starters, Taylor lost none of her underlying sincerity as she evolved from a teenage country star into a sophisticated pop icon. Her lyrics always validated the thoughts and feelings of young women, honoring the cold, hard truth that growing up is messy and full of ups and downs. And her songs never run away from sadness; instead, she tries to make sense of emotional pain and confusion by writing about what she's going through. Even more important, Taylor chronicles life's happier moments too—bonding with your best friend over shared memories ("dorothea") or times when a romance *does* work out and you feel optimistic ("Lover"). Her songs ascribe equal importance to traumatic *and* ecstatic experiences.

Crucially, Taylor realizes that these experiences often produce a complex mix of emotions. The 10-minute version of "All Too Well" is a cathartic song that depicts both the highs and lows of a relationship that ends badly. "The Best Day" is a tearjerker that reminisces about spending wonderful days with your mom. Taylor embraces emotions that swing like a pendulum: Sometimes you want to get blazing revenge on an ex (cue "Picture to Burn" or "Bad Blood"), other times you're uncertain about where you stand in a new relationship (à la "Delicate"), and then you're remembering the delightful private moments of a romance (the wistful "Cornelia Street").

Taylor is also unafraid to explore deeply personal family matters. The somber "Soon You'll Get Better" featuring The Chicks alludes to her mom's real-life health problems, while "marjorie" is a touching homage to Taylor's grandmother, an opera singer.

In 2020, Taylor unveiled a

Red (2012)

1989 (2014)

reputation (2017)

bewitching universe centered on two indie-folk releases: *folklore* and *evermore*. Created during the COVID-19 pandemic with collaborators including The National's Aaron Dessner and Bon Iver's Justin Vernon, the albums are structured like elegant works of fiction with elaborate storylines and vivid characters. "Early in quarantine, I started watching lots of films," she told *Entertainment Weekly* in 2020. "Consuming other people's storytelling opened this portal in my imagination and made me feel like, 'Why have I never created characters and intersecting storylines?'"

Next, Taylor switched it up with her 2022 release, *Midnights*, an album filled with fresh, modern pop textures. Mood-wise, *Midnights* found Taylor feeling vulnerable, candid, and mischievous. She's never been afraid to admit her flaws, but in the anthem "Anti-Hero," Taylor turned inward and blamed herself for her insecurities—a powerful statement that was *deeply* relatable. With 2024's *The Tortured Poets Department*, Taylor released one of her most personal albums yet. Over 31 tracks, she grieves the end of romances—an emotional roller coaster that includes breaking down in tears at the gym ("Down Bad"), reminiscing about a sordid affair ("Fortnight"), and wrestling with harsh realities ("I Can Fix Him (No Really I Can)").

Taylor launched her Eras Tour—a dazzling, dizzying multimedia achievement that became one of the hottest concert (and movie) tickets ever—to celebrate all the albums released since her previous tour. For certain Eras shows, Taylor linked up with the rock trio HAIM to perform a giddy version of their collaborative song "No Body, No Crime," a sinister murder ballad. For Taylor, it was a particularly lovely full-circle moment—going from an aspiring singer belting out The Chicks' "Goodbye Earl" in hopes of launching a career to performing a murder ballad she wrote herself in front of a packed, sold-out stadium.

—ANNIE ZALESKI

Lover (2019)

folklore (2020)

evermore (2020)

In a Vivienne Westwood gown, Taylor sings "But Daddy I Love Him" in Paris in May 2024. Taylor showcased songs from *The Tortured Poets Department* in the second leg of the Eras Tour, a segment which she called "Female Rage: The Musical."

Midnights (2022)

The Tortured Poets Department (2024)

Taylor and HAIM—wearing the gowns from their appearance in Taylor's "Bejeweled" music video—take the stage together for the first-ever live performance of "No Body, No Crime" during the Eras Tour in July 2023. "[Taylor]'s incredibly prolific," Danielle Haim told *People* later that year. "Every time we all get together, we get so excited because we know she's going to play us something new and groundbreaking." The Haim sisters have been friends with Taylor for years and the band opened for Taylor during the 1989 World Tour in 2015.

CERTIFIED   DIAMOND

"THE MAN"

TAYLOR'S VERSIONS

When Taylor's manager Scott Borchetta sold his Big Machine Records to Ithaca Holdings and music manager Scooter Braun without giving Taylor the opportunity to buy back the masters on the first six albums, he fired the first shot in what the the *New York Times* would call "The Pop Music Civil War of 2019."

"For years, I asked, pleaded for a chance to own my work," Taylor wrote on Tumblr in 2019. "Instead I was given an opportunity to sign back up to Big Machine Records and 'earn' one album back at a time, one for every new one I turned in. I walked away because I knew once I signed that contract, Scott Borchetta would sell the label, thereby selling me and my future."

"When I left my masters in Scott's hands, I made peace with the fact that eventually he would sell them," Taylor continued on Tumblr. "Never in my worst nightmares did I imagine the buyer would be Scooter. Any time Scott Borchetta has heard the words 'Scooter Braun' escape my lips, it was when I was either crying or trying not to. He knew what he was doing; they both did. Controlling a woman who didn't want to be associated with them. In perpetuity. That means forever."

When singer Kelly Clarkson heard about the issue in 2019, she tweeted Taylor some terrific advice, writing, 'just a thought, U should go in & re-record all the songs that U don't own the masters on exactly how U did them but put brand new art & some kind of incentive so fans will no longer buy the old versions. I'd buy all of the new versions just to prove a point." Taylor ran with the idea.

Taylor began releasing the revised albums in 2021 through Republic Records to great acclaim and massive sales. She owned the rights to these masters. Her decision marked a departure in the problematic but long-accepted-anyway practices of music ownership and distribution and further solidified her status as a formidable self-advocate.

Taylor and Big Machine Records CEO Scott Borchetta backstage at MetLife Stadium in New Jersey in July 2018. He surprised her with a plaque for *Fearless* reaching Recording Industry Association of America's diamond status, which is 10 millions units sold or streamed.

FROM THE VAULT

(2021)

(2008)

Fearless
(Taylor's Version)
1. You All Over Me
2. Mr. Perfectly Fine
3. We Were Happy
4. That's When
5. Don't You
6. Bye Bye Baby
7. Today Was a Fairytale

Red
(Taylor's Version)
1. Ronan
2. Better Man
3. Nothing New
4. Babe
5. Message in a Bottle
6. I Bet You Think about Me
7. Forever Winter
8. Run
9. The Very First Night
10. All Too Well
   (10-minute version)

(2021)

(2012)

Fans were excited to hear updated versions of their favorite albums, but what many didn't expect was the number of terrific additional "From the Vault" songs that didn't make the cut on the initial album releases. Twenty-six songs from the cutting room floor were added to her first four (*Taylor's Versions*). A number of these songs reached Billboard's Hot 100 chart, including Taylor's *1989* vault track "Is It Over Now?" debuting at number one on November 11, 2023.

(2023)

(2010)

Speak Now
(Taylor's Version)
1. Electric Touch
2. When Emma Falls in Love
3. I Can See You
4. Castles Crumbling
5. Foolish One
6. Timeless

1989
(Taylor's Version)
1. Slut!
2. Say Don't Go
3. Now That We Don't Talk
4. Suburban Legends
5. Is It Over Now?

(2023)

(2014)

At a *Seventeen* photo shoot in 2008.

Ten Years

5 QUESTIONS WITH TAYLOR AT 18

You probably didn't know it in 2008, but Taylor has always been your best friend. She might be a superstar today, but she's also the girl whose jerk boyfriend cheated on her and who wasn't invited to the coolest party of the school year.

Taylor smiles for a photo before performing at the inaugural Academy of Country Music New Artists' Show Party for a Cause, a benefit in Las Vegas on May 14, 2007. The next day, she made her Country Music Awards debut, singing "Tim McGraw" and meeting the man himself.

She was also the one who pined away for that guy who barely noticed her. But back in the day, when every other friend you knew cried it out to their girls or stalked her ex on MySpace, Taylor got out all her sadness, her anger, and her joy in her music. That could explain why her first album, *Taylor Swift*, went double-platinum—because each of her songs sounded so painfully raw and so amazingly honest.

Taylor knew she'd be a star since she was a kid. At age 10, she began her career by performing country music at any kind of event she could in her hometown of Wyomissing, Pennsylvania—karaoke contests, county fairs, wedding receptions, Boy Scouts meetings. By 11, Taylor was handing out homemade demo tapes of her best performances to record executives in Nashville.

When no record labels were interested, she worked harder: She learned how to play the guitar and write her own music—four years later, she finally got signed. But as much as Taylor loved performing, she loved her fans even more. And so she set up her MySpace page, where she played her music, shared

personal photos, and responded to fans' posts herself. Two years and 670,000 MySpace friends later (not to mention three Academy of Country Music award nominations and her sold-out tours), Taylor was a huge success but still an everyday girl. When she was 18, she talked to *Seventeen* about everything she couldn't put into her songs—and why she really hoped you were listening.

Taylor wins the Country Music Association Award for New Artist of the Year—previously known as the Horizon Award—at the November 2007 CMA Awards. "I can't even believe this is real," Taylor says in her acceptance speech. "This is definitely the highlight of my senior year."

Did you ever imagine this would be your life?

I actually started writing in a journal when I was 13. And I have them all in this safe in my house. I have like 25 of them because I would write every single night. It's crazy to go back and read them and think about all these things I once thought were so out of reach. I made this goal sheet when I was like 14 or 15, and it was like, "My life will be complete if . . . I win a CMA [Country Music Association] award, have a platinum record, have a number one song." And I swear to you, one of the goals was to be on the cover of *Seventeen* magazine. So as I'm checking these things off the list, I'm like, 'You're kidding me!'

Did wanting to be a star make it hard for you to relate to the other girls in school?

I think it happens to everybody at some point in her life, where you're completely on the outside of things. It happened to me when I was in seventh grade. I'd been best friends with this group of girls for as long as I could remember, but all of a sudden, they were cool and I wasn't anymore. I didn't look as cool or act as cool as they did, and I couldn't figure out why

they didn't want to hang out with me anymore. And that was really sad, to sit there and wonder, 'What's wrong with me?'

How did you deal?

Well, my mom really became my best friend. I remember when I called those girls early in the day and was like, "Hey, you guys wanna go to the mall?" And they were like, "Oh, no, I've got plans" or "I'm gonna stay home." Everyone had a different excuse. So my mom and I went to the mall—and we ran into all of them hanging out together in a store! I just remember my mom looking at me and saying, "You know what? We're going to go to the King of Prussia Mall!" Which is the best mall in the whole state. We drove an hour to get there, and we had the time of our lives! I realized my mom was the coolest person in the world for not making me stay in that mall and suck it up and go on with things. She let me run from my pain for a little bit, and I thought that was the nicest thing that she ever could have done.

"I want to stay on the road and I want to be headlining. That's my dream."

—TAYLOR, *TAMPA BAY TIMES*, January 2008

Taylor appears at Stagecoach, California's three-day Country Music Festival, in May 2008, featuring some of her heroes: Tim McGraw, Carrie Underwood, Trisha Yearwood, Luke Bryan, and George Jones.

Taylor sings "I Should've Said No" at the May 2008 ACM Awards. She reflected after the performance on MySpace: "I've always wanted to perform an angry song and have water rain down from the ceiling and have a little freakout onstage."

So did you make new friends?

I flew solo for a while. But then my family felt like it might be really cool to change scenery, so we moved to a town outside Nashville. But I think about it this way: If I had been popular, I wouldn't have wanted to leave. If I hadn't wanted to leave, then I wouldn't be sitting here doing an interview for a *Seventeen* magazine cover!

True! Did you ever hear from those girls again?

I was actually playing a sold-out show in my hometown, and I was signing autographs afterward. And I saw those girls who didn't invite me to their parties and didn't invite me to hang out with them. They waited in line for three hours to say hi to me. They were each wearing a T-shirt with my face on it, asking me to sign it for them! That's where I have to look at this situation and say, "We were kids." And at some point, you have to forget about grudges because they only hurt. And you realize you got good songs about being alone, and you got through it.

—**CARISSA ROSENBERG TOZZI**

Taylor and her mom, Andrea, admire her nomination for Top Female Vocalist at the Academy of Country Music Awards in May 2008. While she didn't win that category, Taylor won the award for Best New Artist. She thanked her mom in her acceptance speech for leaving home "to go on the road with her 16-year-old daughter. Then she was sleeping in rental cars and in airplanes with her mouth hanging wide open 'cause she was so tired. And so, Mom, thank you so much. I love you. This is for you."

Taylor poses with manager Scott Borchetta and his wife, Sandy, at the April 2008 CMT Awards in Nashville. Borchetta had signed Taylor at age 14 to his new record company after seeing her perform at the storied Bluebird Cafe in 2003. "He didn't have a name for [Big Machine Records]," Taylor told *CMT Insider*. "He didn't have a building for it. And he didn't have staff for it. But he had a dream and [asked] would I come on board? I went with my gut instinct, which just said, 'Say yes.'"

Taylor makes her American Music Awards musical debut in November 2008 with the song "White Horse." Later that night, she beat out Carrie Underwood and Reba McEntire to win Favorite Country Female Artist.

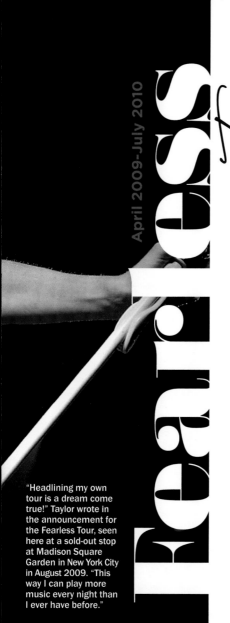

Fearless Tour

Taylor embarked on her first headlining tour upon the release of *Fearless*. The 15-month trek took her all over the world. The tour, which featured multiple costume changes, visual elements designed by Taylor, and a fairy-tale castle that was said to be illumined by more than a million lumens of light, also nabbed the Top Package Award at Billboard's 2010 Touring Awards.

"Headlining my own tour is a dream come true!" Taylor wrote in the announcement for the Fearless Tour, seen here at a sold-out stop at Madison Square Garden in New York City in August 2009. "This way I can play more music every night than I ever have before."

BY THE NUMBERS

118 shows
1.14M fans attended
$66.5M grossed

BELOW: Taylor wows crowds in New York City in an ornate ball gown for her performance of "Love Story." She wanted to make her Fearless Tour a spectacle. "My favorite thing when I go to a concert is having lots of changing things to look at," she wrote of the tour, "so I've been working really hard to make this show as multi-dimensional as possible." **RIGHT:** Taylor wins so many awards for *Fearless* at the February 2010 Grammys that she accidentally drops one. *Fearless* is the only full-length country album to ever win a Grammy Award for Album of the Year and Country Album of the Year from the American Music Awards, Country Music Association, and Academy of Country Music Awards.

For her first Grammy performance in February 2009, Taylor duets with close friend Miley Cyrus on Taylor's song "Fifteen." Miley tells reporters on the red carpet, "I was sitting in the chair doing my makeup and I said, 'Taylor, I really love you. I am so happy we are friends.'"

At a *Seventeen*
photo shoot in 2009.

TAYLOR'S THOUGHTS ON RELATIONSHIPS

She was 19 and her life seemed like a fairy tale. A sweet, talented girl from a small town in Pennsylvania gets discovered and is soon anointed the Princess of Pop Country. Then, when she joins the Jonas Brothers on tour, she meets her Prince Charming—aka Joe Jonas. They travel across the country to see one another, appear in the front row of each other's concerts, and attend MTV's VMAs together. But one fall afternoon, she gets a 27-second phone call from him saying it's over.

Only the story doesn't end there—it's where it starts to get good. After Taylor vented her frustration by joking about the breakup in her *Saturday Night Live* monologue, the 19-year-old turned those tough love lessons into great songs. Every single track on her next number one album, *Fearless*, was based on a personal experience.

And then Taylor proceeded to take over the world. She designed a line of sundresses for L.e.i., which were available at Walmart; performed at the World Series and the Grammys; had a guest-starring role on *CSI*; and set a new music record—"Love Story" was the first country song ever to reach number one on the Top 40 pop chart. And as the ultimate proof that she was a major star, she headlined her first tour, filling tens of thousands of seats in stadiums across the country.

She opened up in 2009 to *Seventeen* about why she's a hopeless romantic and what she's truly learned from heartbreak.

What's your favorite thing to write songs about?

Right now, my favorite thing to write about is love. And breakups. And boys. And feelings. Honesty is a big part of my writing, because when I was younger and fell in love with songs I'd hear, I would always wonder who that song was about. It would have totally broken my heart to know it wasn't about anyone and was just written so it could be on the radio.

Joe Jonas and Taylor attend the September 2008 MTV VMA awards as a couple. After Jonas breaks up with her a month later on a 27-second phone call, Taylor addresses the split with humor in "The Monologue Song (La, La, La)" while hosting *Saturday Night Live* in November 2009. "You might think I'd bring up Joe, that guy who broke up with me on the phone . . ." she sings with an eye roll. "But I'm not gonna mention him in my monologue."

You wrote "Forever and Always" about your breakup with Joe Jonas. Do you regret putting those emotions out there?

Writing songs about people is the only way I know how to do things. I mean, I can't wish I hadn't written a song about someone, because if I hadn't, that song wouldn't exist. I just don't find any joy in writing about things I haven't been through.

But why do you focus on the difficult stuff?

The hardest thing about heartbreak is feeling like you're alone, and that the other person doesn't really care. But when you hear a song about it, you realize you're not alone—because the person who wrote it went through the same thing. That's why songs about heartbreak are so relatable. When you miss somebody and you hear a happy song, it just makes you mad.

Isn't getting mad part of the breakup process?

I think getting mad is always your first reaction when something hurts. And you shouldn't feel bad about that. Every person you date is different and makes you feel differently. Sometimes you can shake it off and you're fine —and then with another person it can really affect you. It's the unpredictability of love that really scares us, but it's also what draws us to it.

So how do you let go and move on?

I think that you never fully let go of everything. And that should be your goal, because you can take away something good from everything that happens to you.

What is your biggest fear in life?

Being accused of a crime I didn't commit. [Laughs.] I have nightmares about it. In the dream, I don't even know what I'm being accused of, but the police are coming after me with handcuffs while my mom is crying and asking where she went wrong. I'm screaming, "I didn't do it!" but no one can hear me. It's my only recurring dream, and it freaks me out.

That is freaky! Do you have a close group of girlfriends that you always rely on to get you through a hard time?

In Nashville, it's Abigail [who's mentioned in Taylor's song "Fifteen"] and Kellie Pickler. In LA, Selena Gomez is one of my best friends. I'm also really close with Miley [Cyrus], Demi Lovato, and Emma Stone.

LEFT: Taylor peeks out of her tour bus in October 2009. Since she spends so much of her career on the road, she designs the buses to be both beautiful and practical. For example, her *Fearless* bus had a chandelier and a drop-down treadmill. **RIGHT:** Taylor supports her friend and actress Emma Stone at the *Easy A* premiere in September 2010. The two met after Emma sent Taylor an email saying she liked her music, Taylor told MTV, "and then we started talking and hanging out." Their friendship has stood the test of time. Stone attended three nights of the Eras Tour, including the opening show in her hometown of Glendale, Arizona.

What kind of stuff do you guys talk about?

Talking to my friends about their dating lives is my number one hobby. Which is really ironic, because when I go to them and ask, "What should I do?" they're like, "I don't know!" And I'm like, "When you and your boyfriend were fighting, I talked to you for two hours and told you all those things! Remember?!?"

What would you say is your biggest love "don't"?

No one wants to be with someone who desperately needs them. You should want the other person and love him, but you shouldn't need him. If you depend on him for your happiness, that's not good, because what will you do when it ends?

What's the secret to a good relationship?

Here's my theory: If you end up lasting with someone for years and years, eventually you'll run out of things to talk about or find out about each other. So you'd better pick a person who can make you laugh about nothing, or who can pull conversations out of the air.

Are you dating anyone right now?

No, I'm perpetually single. If I meet someone who is really great, I'll date him. But I've had those friends who have to have a boyfriend all the time, and as soon as it doesn't work out with one, they jump to another one within 24 hours. What would happen if you were stuck in a relationship with

63

someone who wasn't right for you, just because you were lonely—and then missed meeting Mr. Right? Being alone is not the same as being lonely.

What do you mean?
When you're alone, you're going to have lonely moments, but it's important to be happy with yourself. Sure, you'll always feel a little weird being alone on Valentine's Day, but you can't let that force you into a relationship with a guy you're not supposed to be with.

So what do you do when you're alone?
I like to do things that glorify being alone. I buy a candle that smells pretty, turn down the lights, and make a playlist of low-key songs. If you don't act like you've been hit by the plague when you're alone on Friday night, and just see it as a chance to have fun by yourself, it's not a bad day.

What traits do you look for in a guy?
It would be unfair to have a general

rule for every guy because they're all individual stories, not just chapters in one big book. But the guy I'm looking for is the guy I can be me around, not a version of me I think he'd like. He's the guy I'm not wearing different clothes for. I'm not holding back jokes because he might think they're stupid. I'm not afraid to show emotion because I might scare him. It's important to not have rules about who the guy is: The rule should be about who you are when you're with him.

How do you think you find that guy?

You can't predict who you'll fall in love with. Love's the one thing that doesn't have a pattern—it's a total mystery. If you overthink it, you're wasting your time.

Can real-life love be as good as a fairy tale?

I have to believe in fairy tales, and I have to believe in love—but not blindly. If you do meet Prince Charming, know he is going to have his good days and his bad days. He is going to have days when his hair looks horrible, and days when he's moody and says something that hurts your feelings. You have to base your fairy tale not upon happily ever after, but on happy right now.

—HOLLY C. CORBETT

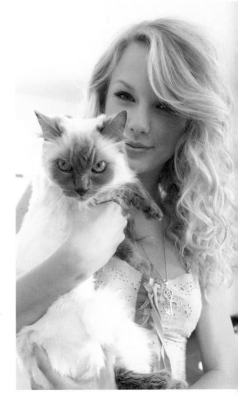

LEFT: Taylor performs her hit "Love Story" at the CMA Awards in November 2008. She wrote the song in 20 minutes, and it went on to spend 49 weeks on the Billboard Hot 100 chart, peaking at number four in 2009. **BELOW:** Taylor poses with a feline friend at an *US Weekly* shoot in September 2008. Three years later, she adopted her first cat, Meredith Grey, a Scottish Fold named after her favorite *Grey's Anatomy* character. She has since adopted two more: Olivia Benson and Benjamin Button.

"INNOCENT"

KANYE DRAMA

At the 2009 MTV Video Music Awards, Taylor won the award for Best Female Video for her unrequited love anthem "You Belong with Me." During her speech, Kanye West jumped on the stage and grabbed the mic, interrupting with the now-immortal words: "Yo, Taylor, I'm really happy for you and I'mma let you finish, but Beyoncé had one of the best videos of all time. One of the best videos of all time!" After he left the stage, a speechless Taylor was escorted off.

"My overall thought process was something like:

'Wow, I can't believe I won, this is awesome,

don't trip and fall,

this is so cool.

Oh, Kanye West is here.

Cool haircut.

What are you doing there?'

And then, 'Ouch.' And then, 'I guess I'm not gonna get to thank the fans.'"

said Taylor, describing the incident on The View.

In 2015, Taylor, West, and his then–wife Kim Kardashian hung out at the Grammys, and later that year, Taylor presented Kanye with the Video Vanguard Award at his request at the VMAs. But in 2016, Kanye debuted a new track, "Famous," with the lyrics, "I feel like me and Taylor might still have sex / Why? I made that bitch famous." He also released a video showing a wax figure of Taylor naked next to him in bed.

West said Taylor shouldn't have been surprised because he had called her about the song. Taylor's camp said they had spoken, but she didn't know the lyrics. Kardashian said Taylor was lying and released an excerpt of their video call. Their fans began posting snake emojis all over Taylor's social media with the hashtag #TaylorIsASnake. At this point, she stopped trying to make sense of Kanye.

PREVIOUS SPREAD: Taylor looks confused as Kanye joins her onstage at the MTV Video Music Awards. **LEFT:** Taylor does get her chance to thank fans at the 2009 MTV Video Music Awards when Beyoncé generously invites her onto the stage during her acceptance speech for Video of the Year for "Single Ladies (Put a Ring on It)." "I remember being 17 years old, up for my first MTV Award with Destiny's Child," Beyoncé said. "It was one of the most exciting moments in my life. So, I'd like for Taylor to come out and have her moment."

At a *Cosmopolitan* photo shoot in 2012.

Speak Now Tour

With *Speak Now*, Taylor realized that she had the power to control some of the narrative about herself with her lyrics, which she wrote on her own during her extensive tour for *Fearless*. Debuting at number one on the Billboard charts, the album quieted the critics, who had given too much credit to her cowriters on previous albums. She told *New York Magazine* that she selected the album's title "because I think it's a metaphor for so many things we go through in life, that moment where it's almost too late, and you've gotta either say what it is you are feeling or deal with the consequences forever." The tour covered 110 shows in the Americas, Asia, Europe, and Oceania and was the highest-grossing by a female artist in 2011.

Taylor serenades a sold-out crowd of more than 51,000 fans in Pennsylvania in August 2011 during the Speak Now World Tour. At each stop she played surprise cover songs: In Philadelphia, Taylor added "Who Knew" by Pink and "Unpretty" by TLC.

BY THE NUMBERS

110 shows
1.1M fans attended
$123.7M grossed

BELOW: Taylor purchases her album *Speak Now* alongside fans at the Times Square Starbucks in New York City in October 2010. While the coffee chain stopped selling CDs in 2015, they have continued to collaborate with Taylor, even adding a "Taylor's Latte" to their menu during their holiday "red cup season" to celebrate the release of *Red (Taylor's Version)* in November 2021. **RIGHT:** Taylor celebrates with pal Selena Gomez after winning Artist of the Year at the November 2011 AMAs. They became friends in 2008 when they were each dating a Jonas brother. While those relationships didn't last, Taylor and Selena stayed close. "We've had so many things in our lives that have changed over the past couple of years," Taylor later told *Access Hollywood* in 2012, "but our friendship has stayed the same."

ABOVE: Taylor has a number of musical inspirations. Here she performs "You Belong with Me" and "Rhiannon" with one of her idols, Stevie Nicks, at the 2010 Grammys. She was a little off-key, and one critic's take was that she "can't sing" and that she's "too young and dumb to understand the mistake she made" by not using auto-tune. She responded in songwriter fashion, penning the pointed "Mean." **BELOW:** Taylor sings alongside (left to right) Hillary Scott, Charles Kelley, Faith Hill, and Dave Haygood at the Country Music Hall of Fame benefit in October 2009. Taylor met Faith Hill in 2007 and considers her a mentor.

Taylor beams in the company of James Taylor while performing her song "Fire and Rain" in November 2011 on her Speak Now World Tour. Named after the musician, she yelled out, "Tell James Taylor I love him!" when Jack Antonoff called her from the stage to let her know they had won for Best Pop Vocal Album during the 2016 Grammys.

Taylor closes the November 2012 MTV Europe Music Awards in Germany with a showstopping circus-themed performance of "We Are Never Ever Getting Back Together" from her album *Red*. Earlier that night, she won three EMAs, for Best Female, Best Live, and Best Look.

Red Tour

March 2013—June 2014

Taylor continued to be a record-setting concert draw. **Billboard** notes the Red Tour "smashed the all-time revenue record for a single tour by a country artist." Coincidentally, the previous country tour record was held by Tim McGraw and Faith Hill's Soul2Soul II Tour, during which Taylor herself opened some dates.

BY THE NUMBERS

86 shows
1.7M fans attended
$150.2M grossed

BELOW: In August 2013, Taylor receives a plaque from the Staples Center in Los Angeles for breaking the record for the most sold-out shows there for a solo artist (11). Britney Spears previously held the record with 8 shows. **RIGHT:** Taylor dazzles at the December 2012 Z100 Jingle Ball. With a microphone matching her signature red lipstick, she belts out *Red*'s hits including "State of Grace," "I Knew You Were Trouble," "We're Never Ever Getting Back Together," and duets with Ed Sheeran on "Everything Has Changed." The *New York Times* later wrote of her performance, "The boss was in the house."

TAYLOR
ON FRIENDS
AND FAME

Esquire writer Scott Raab met Taylor for breakfast in downtown Manhattan in 2014, a few days before her massive hit single "Shake It Off" was released. She was coming from a promotional photo shoot and, after breakfast, was heading to Los Angeles to rehearse for the Video Music Awards later that same afternoon. Her publicity manager and two bodyguards were seated at a table nearby. For Taylor: scrambled eggs, no coffee.

At a *Cosmopolitan* photo shoot in 2012.

It's 8:30 A.M. and you've already been working for two hours?
We were at the Empire State Building because we're shooting for the live stream on Monday. There will be a wide helicopter camera shot on the Empire State Building, and I will be up on the top platform waving. It's so exciting to unveil who you've been for the last two years. My life has changed drastically in the last year and a half.

Musically? Geographically?
Everything. I never thought I'd live in New York, because I thought I'd be too overwhelmed by how busy and bright and crazy the city is. Then all of a sudden, this year, all I wanted to do was live in New York. I never thought I would be so happy being completely unattached to anyone romantically.

Why do you think there's so much attention paid to your dating habits?
I think with every celebrity story there has to be a "Yeah, but . . ." Take Beyoncé: She's incredibly talented, gorgeous, [a] perfect role model for girls, empowering women all over the world. Yeah, but . . . let's try to pick at her marriage. I think that every celebrity has that. And predominantly women, unfortunately.

Taylor attends the August 2015 VMA after-party at Republic Records in West Hollywood with her "Bad Blood" squad, including Martha Hunt, Lily Aldridge, Selena Gomez, Hailee Steinfeld, and Serayah McNeill. Three years later, Republic would be her new label as she would be able to retain the rights to her future masters there.

You're judged constantly. Your private life is clickbait.

I would date someone, figure out we weren't compatible or figure out we didn't work out, and then we'd break up. That seems like a very normal thing for a young 20-something to do, and that is my biggest scandal. I think it's healthy for everyone to go a few years without dating, just because you need to get to know who you are. And I've done more thinking and examining and figuring out how to cope with things on my own than I would have if I had been focusing on someone else's emotions and someone else's schedule. It's been really good.

I think I was watching an *Ellen* clip—it might have been Chelsea Handler—and she's teasing you, and at one point you said, "No one listens to me!" And it wasn't that you were that aggravated, but it stuck in my head because I think that's true: No one's actually paying attention to the human there.

It doesn't seem like a possibility at this point in my life. What does seem possible and easy and comfortable is having this entire league of incredible girlfriends that I have. And I can trust them, and the reason I know I can trust them is because nothing true about me is being written in the press right now.

You knew what your passion was early. It must take an incredible amount of energy to sustain that passion.

I'm very busy, and I'm tired a lot. I was talking to [songwriter-producer] Ryan Tedder about this the other day, because we're both equal left- and right-brain people. So there's part of our brain that we shut off when we're in the studio. There's part of our brain that we turn on when we are out doing an interview or promoting something or waking up at six in the morning for hair and makeup. I think if that pressure came from other people, I would feel very weighed down by it. But the pressure comes from me, so I can't really say anything about it, because I'm the one saying to myself, *You have to make a better album than you made last time. There is no other option. Otherwise, don't make an album.*

I know that you have an infrastructure with family and all that, but do you ever feel like it's a runaway train?

No. The only thing I can't control is the spin in the press. And so if I know I can't control that, I have to let it go. In some ways, though, you can control it. I really didn't like the whole serial-dater thing. I thought it was a really sexist angle on my life. And so I just stopped dating people, because it meant a lot to me to set the record straight—that I do not need some guy around in order to get inspiration, in order to make a great record, in order to live my life, in order to feel okay about myself. And I wanted to show my fans the same thing.

You have your own jet?

Yeah, isn't that crazy?

You still do the meet-and-greets?

We do four before the show and one after.

That's country music, where it's not just about the songs.

Country music teaches you to work. You hear stories about these artists who show up four hours late to a photo shoot,

and in Nashville that doesn't happen. In Nashville, if you go four hours late to a photo shoot, everyone leaves. In Nashville, if you don't care about radio and being kind to the people who are being good to you . . . It's a symbiotic relationship, and if you don't take care of it, then they won't take care of you. I've never been more proud to have come from a community that's so rooted in songwriting, so rooted in hard work and in treating people well. It was the best kind of training.

I've read about you writing thank-you notes to deejays.

I love writing thank-you notes. There's something very nostalgic to me about the feel of a card and putting pen to paper. How many times in our lives are we required to put pen to paper anymore?

I haven't written anyone a letter in years.

There's something romantic and sort of lost about it. I like things you can touch and things you can keep, because every bit of communication we have is ephemeral in nature. You can just delete an e-mail and it's like it was never there.

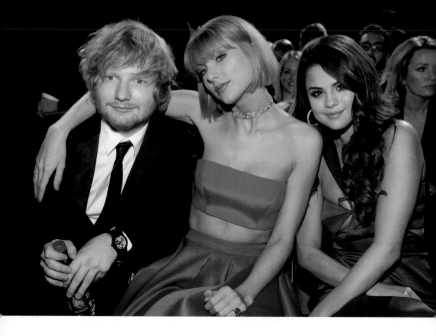

You seem utterly sane.
Thank you.

I mistrust that somehow.
You don't need to be cynical about it!

It's not you. It's my job.
That's what I don't like about celebrity culture and the obsession with it, and the takedown culture that we seem to be in. You have celebrities who are pushed to the brink of a public meltdown, and so the public thinks that every person in the public eye has dirty secrets that they're keeping, or isn't what they seem, or is masking it and faking sincerity, faking authenticity, faking being surprised at award shows when you win a Grammy.

There's a certain cruelty to it. When the meltdown does happen, people couldn't be more thrilled, especially if it's a young woman.
I'm not gonna let them make me have a meltdown. But, I think, as a songwriter you lose your edge if you find a way to protect yourself from everything they're going to say about you. You lose touch with what made you vulnerable enough to connect with people in your songwriting. And that's not something I wanna do. So it's all about walking a tightrope between not being so fragile and breakable that they can level you with one blow and being raw enough to feel it and write about it when you feel it. And it's not just a celebrity

BFFs Ed Sheeran, Taylor, and Selena Gomez sit together at the Grammy Awards in February 2016, where *1989* won Album of the Year. Sheeran's favorite song on the album was "Bad Blood," which he thought should have been the first single instead of "Shake it Off."

takedown culture. It's a takedown culture. I know it when I see these kids —they're gonna get tortured socially until they find their calling in life.

You went through that kind of thing yourself in school.

I never felt like the kids in school were right about me when they'd say, "She's weird. She's annoying. I don't want to hang out with her." I always remember writing in my journal, "I just have to keep writing songs. I just have to keep doing this and someday, maybe, this will be different for me. I just have to keep working."

They seem like nice guys, your bodyguards.

They're really nice. They're incredible.

I've never interviewed anyone who brought security.

I fought the idea of having security for a very long time, because I really value normalcy. I really do. I like to be able to take a drive by myself. Haven't done that in six years.

Even in Tennessee?

No, they have to be in a car behind me. Because just the sheer number of men we have in a file who have showed up at my house, showed up at my mom's house, threatened to either kill me, kidnap me, or marry me. This is the strange and sad part of my life that I try not to think about. I try to be lighthearted about it, because I don't ever want to be scared. I don't want to be walking down the street scared. And when I have security, I don't have to be scared.

Do you still have connections with human beings?

It's a social situation every time I go out, but if I know I can't deal with talking to people that day, I just don't go out. I just have to wake up in the morning and say, "How am I feeling today?" If someone asks for a picture, am I gonna feel imposed upon today because I'm dealing with my own stuff? Am I gonna take my own stuff out on some innocent 14-year-old today and be in a bad mood? Okay, maybe not . . . Maybe I won't leave the house. I try really hard not to take bad days out on other people. Because I *will* get asked for an autograph, and I *will* get asked for a picture, and there *will* be someone with their cell phone filming me at a restaurant. If I'm not

Taylor and supermodel Karlie Kloss take to the runway at their second Victoria's Secret Runway Show. They became fast friends after appearing together on the runway in 2013 and are later spotted together so often that rumors begin to circulate that they are an item. After the 2014 runway show, Taylor posted a request on Instagram: "As my 25th birthday present from the media, I'd like for you to stop accusing all my friends of dating me."

in the mood for that, I just kind of stay in. And that's fine. Those days don't happen very often. I try really hard to keep it light. Joy, enthusiasm, excitement—those are sort of my chief attributes.

I read that you finished two years of high school in 12 months.

That was just the most practical way to do it.

But not everyone could do it.

My parents were very strict about education and hard work, from the time my brother and I were really little kids.

You and your family lived on a Christmas tree farm? That's a unique place to grow up.

It was such a weird place to grow up. But it has cemented in me this unnatural level of excitement about fall and then the holiday season. My friends are so sick of me talking about autumn coming. They're like, "What are you, an elf?"

Who took care of the tree business?

My dad.

I thought he was a Merrill Lynch guy.

He'd tend to the farm as his hobby. He'd get up four hours early to go mow the fields on his tractor. We all had jobs. Mine was picking the praying-mantis pods off of the trees, collecting them so that the bugs wouldn't hatch inside people's houses.

How old were you?

From 5 to 10. The only reason that was my job was because I was too little to help lift trees.

You've mentioned your grandmother in past interviews. What kind of singing did she do?

She sang opera. She would sing in whatever city opera production when my grandfather was working. He was an engineer and he would travel a lot, building bridges. She even was a cohost on this show called *The Pan American Show*, in Puerto Rico, and she was beautiful and graceful but spoke the worst Spanish you've ever heard. All the Spanish-speaking fans in Puerto Rico just loved her, because she was so brave about how terrible she was at speaking Spanish. She tried every night. And then she'd get

up and sing, and, of course, it was the perfect, beautiful operatic voice. Gorgeous soprano.

Have you seen yourself in *The Giver*? [Taylor had a cameo as Rosemary, a previous Receiver of Memory].

I saw the movie. It's hard for me to separate myself from myself. I just see me in a brown wig and I think, *Oh, I look so weird there. Why does my face look so weird? Oh, I hate the sound of my voice.* Music is the only thing that's ever fit me like that little black dress you wear every single time you go out. Other things fit me for certain seasons, but music is the only thing that I would wear all year round. *[To her manager]* Can I play him something? So this is the first single—this is about the most important lesson I've learned in the last couple of years. *["Shake It Off" plays through earbuds.]* Well, that's that.

Nice. I think you're gonna be big.

Thank you!

Taylor's *Great Gatsby*–themed performance of "Shake It Off," at the MTV Video Music Awards in August 2014 featured a full band and dancers from the era. The hit song debuted at number one on Billboard's Hot 100 chart and stayed in the top 10 on that chart for nearly six months.

You have a great sense of humor, but you keep it kind of hidden. It's self-effacing and a little sarcastic, but you use it very judiciously.

I think it's nice to have some tricks up your sleeve. Everybody sees every part of everything I do, and they all draw their own conclusions from it, so there has to be a little bit of you that people only get when they're in person with you.

Do you ever feel trapped in the persona of sweetness, innocence, purity?

No, because I'm realistic about the fact that millions of people don't have time in their day to maintain a complex profile of who I am. They're busy with their work and their kids and their husband or their boyfriend and their friends. They only have time to come up with about two or three adjectives to describe people in the public eye. And that's okay. As long as those three adjectives aren't *train wreck, mess, terrible*. I figure eventually, if you hang around long enough, people will see all sides of you.

More evidence of your sanity.

When I was a little kid, my friends were watching Disney Channel, but I was watching *Behind the Music*. And I was drawing these conclusions, like the reason these people went off the rails is because they lost their level of self-awareness. They turned a blind eye to things they didn't want to see, and all of a sudden all they were seeing were their delusions of grandeur. And I never wanted to make that mistake in my life, regardless of what my career ended up being. I take away these kind of life lessons from that show.

You've thought about this.

I have a lot of time. That's all I do.

—SCOTT RAAB

1989 *Tour*

Taylor wanted to add an element of surprise to her massive 1989 World Tour for her social media–savvy fans. "They know the set list. They know the costumes. They've looked it up. That presented me with an interesting issue," she said in a Beats 1 interview. She opened up her Rolodex of celebrity friends and added special guests to each stop, including icons like Mary J. Blige, Mick Jagger, and Kobe Bryant, as well as less obvious choices like Lena Dunham and Matt LeBlanc.

Taylor opens her 1989 World Tour with "Welcome to New York" and ended with a confetti-popping dance to "Shake It Off" on a rotating stage at this August 2015 stop in Los Angeles. *Pollstar* and iHeartRadio awarded the show best tour in 2016.

BY THE NUMBERS

85 shows
2.2M fans attended
$250.7M grossed

"WILDEST DREAMS"

THE MET GALA

2008

Taylor stepped out in a big way at her first Met Gala in 2008 in a long Badgley Mischka gown in different shades of gold and prominent drop earrings. In a nod to the theme of "Superheroes: Fashion and Fantasy," the look felt very She-Ra: Princess of Power or fierce Greek goddess. Below she navigates the stairs with designer James Mischka.

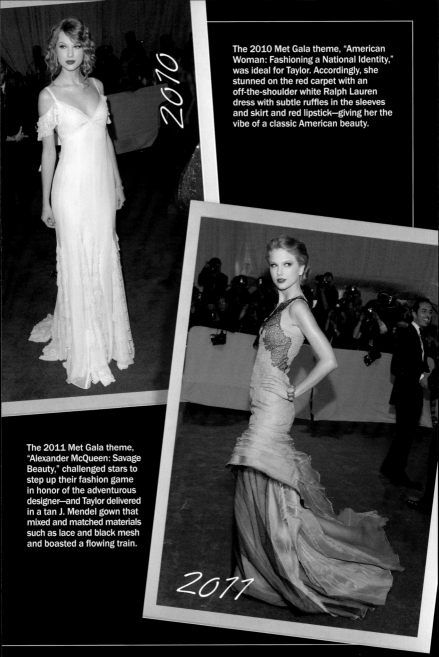

2010

The 2010 Met Gala theme, "American Woman: Fashioning a National Identity," was ideal for Taylor. Accordingly, she stunned on the red carpet with an off-the-shoulder white Ralph Lauren dress with subtle ruffles in the sleeves and skirt and red lipstick—giving her the vibe of a classic American beauty.

The 2011 Met Gala theme, "Alexander McQueen: Savage Beauty," challenged stars to step up their fashion game in honor of the adventurous designer—and Taylor delivered in a tan J. Mendel gown that mixed and matched materials such as lace and black mesh and boasted a flowing train.

2011

Taylor went for edgy at the 2013 Met Gala in a note-perfect nod to the theme "PUNK: Chaos to Couture." She wore a black J. Mendel gown with a striking silhouette, geometric cutouts, and a dazzling bejeweled neckline—and paired this with smoky eye makeup.

2013

The 2014 Met Gala's theme, "Charles James: Beyond Fashion," honored the designer who was known for his formal gowns. Fittingly, Taylor looked like a glam vintage Hollywood starlet, thanks to a light pink Oscar de la Renta dress with a dramatic train and bow, a wavy hairdo, and her trademark striking red lip.

2014

Taylor cochaired the 2016 Met Gala and sported a futuristic outfit befitting the "Manus x Machina: Fashion in an Age of Technology" theme: a silver Louis Vuitton dress with a flared skirt and peekaboo cutouts. She paired the dress with lace-up sandals (left), dark lipstick, and a sleek, platinum-blonde bob— exuding a space-age robotic vibe.

2016

Reputation Tour

Tour

After the public feud with Kanye and Kim, Taylor took a break from the media and regrouped emotionally. "I don't think that there are that many people who can actually understand what it's like to have millions of people hate you very loudly," she told *InStyle*. She returned with the release of *reputation* and the tour, which was considered by many critics to be the best of 2018.

·BY THE NUMBERS·

53 shows
2.9M fans attended
$345M grossed

Taylor greets fans in November 2018 in Brisbane, Australia, during her Reputation Tour. The release of the album and tour were "the most transformative emotional experience of my career," Taylor told *Rolling Stone*. ". . . After that tour, bad stuff can happen to me, but it doesn't level me anymore."

Taylor teams up with Panic at the Disco's Brendon Urie for her song "ME!," which the pair performed to open the May 2019 Billboard Music Awards in Las Vegas. Taylor changed the lyrics to fit the occasion, turning the song's catchy "Spelling is fun!" to "Vegas is fun!"

Lover

CANCELED Tour

August 2020

Lover, released in 2019, was the first album for which Taylor owned the masters. She told *Vogue* that "it is really a love letter to love, in all of its maddening, passionate, exciting, enchanting, horrific, tragic, wonderful glory." Taylor planned to launch her Lover Fest tour in 2020. After the tour was postponed due to the pandemic, she finally had to cancel, writing on her social media, "This is an unprecedented pandemic that has changed everyone's plans and no one knows what the touring landscape is going to look like in the near future. I'm so disappointed that I won't be able to see you in person as soon as I wanted to."

103

In August 2019, Taylor surprises fans with an appearance at a Spotify mural in Brooklyn featuring the "angels roll their eyes" lyrics from *Lover*'s "Cruel Summer." She later posted on social media: "Had to go see the mural in person and it turns out she's GLORIOUS."

Taylor performs at L'Olympia in Paris, during the "City of Lover Concert," in 2019. Taylor postponed and then canceled most of her Lover Fest tour dates due to the pandemic, and released a recording of the concert, which had been filmed before a small audience, on ABC in May 2020. In it, Taylor shared details behind the songs like "Cornelia Street" ("I think I wrote this song actually, like, when I was in the bathtub") and "Lover" ("I just went to the piano, stumbled over to the piano, sat down and this song happened so quick").

At the 2022 Toronto
International Film Festival.

30s

Taylor performs "betty" from *folklore* live for the first time at the September 2020 Academy of Country Music Awards at the Grand Ole Opry, her first AMC performance in seven years. It's one of the three songs depicting an imagined love triangle, along with "cardigan" and "august." Taylor wrote the song with then-boyfriend Joe Alwyn, which she said helped her with the male perspective.

"*Songwriting on this album is exactly the way that I would write if I considered nothing else other than, 'What words do I want to write? What stories do I want to tell?'*"

—**TAYLOR,** *ENTERTAINMENT WEEKLY,* December 2020

BELOW: Taylor smiles in front of a display at the Golden Globe Awards promoting the movie *Cats* in January 2020 in which she appeared as Bombalurina. She also cowrote "Beautiful Ghosts" with Andrew Lloyd Webber for the film, which earned her her third Golden Globe nomination for Best Original Song. "I have cats. I'm obsessed with them. I love my cats so much that when a role came up in a movie called *Cats*, I just thought, like, I gotta do this," she told *Time* in 2019. **RIGHT:** *folklore* collaborators Jack Antonoff, left, and Bryce Dessner pose with Taylor at the 63rd Annual Grammy Awards in March 2021, where they performed a medley of "cardigan," "august," and "willow." This was Taylor's seventh time performing at the Grammys.

BELOW: Taylor and then-boyfriend Joe Alwyn attend the January 2020 Golden Globe Awards together. The couple cowrote some songs on *folklore,* with Alwyn working under the alias William Bowery. He talked about the creative process during an interview with *The Guardian*. "It came about from messing around on a piano and singing badly, then being overheard and being like, 'Let's see what happens if we get to the end of it together.'" When *folklore* won Album of the Year at the 2021 Grammy Awards, Taylor thanked him. "Joe, who is the first person that I play every single song that I write, and I had the best time writing songs with you in quarantine," she said. **LEFT:** Taylor was nominated for six awards at the March 2021 Grammys. While accepting the Album of the Year award for *folklore*, Taylor thanked fans in her speech. "You guys met us in this imaginary world that we created, and we can't tell you how honored we are forever by this." It is the third time she took home this prestigious award, making her the fourth artist—and the first woman ever—to achieve this feat.

Taylor drops by for a surprise Pride Month performance with Jesse Tyler Ferguson at the Stonewall Inn, the legendary gay bar in New York City, in June 2019. "I heard this is Jesse's favorite song to do at karaoke," she said, before breaking into "Shake It Off." The day before, Taylor had released her single "You Need to Calm Down," which has shout-outs to the LGBTQ+ community.

5 LESSONS

FROM A LIFETIME IN THE

SPOTLIGHT

"Part of growing up and moving into new chapters of your life is about catch and release," said Taylor during her 2022 commencement address at New York University (NYU). "Decide what is yours to hold and let the rest go." For Taylor, who has been onstage since she was 10 years old, that means putting her precious time and energy into the people and projects that matter and being strong enough to filter out what's not serving her goals.

To that end, Taylor has spent her early 30s communicating directly to her fans, imparting what she knows is true. Whether through posts to her more than 500 million followers on social media, the documentary *Miss Americana*, or connecting with Swifties at every stop of the Eras Tour, she's taken firm control of the narrative that surrounds her. Along the way, Taylor shared a few hard-won lessons.

1

Put Other People's Opinions in Perspective
"I learned not to let outside opinions establish the value I place on my own life choices," Taylor told *Elle* in 2019. "For too long, the projected opinions of strangers affected how I viewed my relationships. Whether it was the general internet consensus of who would be right for me, or what they thought was 'couples goals' based on a picture I posted on Instagram. That stuff isn't real. For an approval seeker like me, it was an important lesson for me to learn to have my *own* value system of what I actually want."

Stand Up for What You Know Is Right

"Rights are being stripped from basically everyone who isn't a straight white cisgender male," Taylor told *Vogue* in 2019 about standing up for LGBTQ+ rights. "I didn't realize until recently that I could advocate for a community that I'm not a part of. It's hard to know how to do that without being so fearful of making a mistake that you just freeze. Because my mistakes are very loud. When I make a mistake, it echoes through the canyons of the world. It's clickbait, and it's a part of my life story, and it's a part of my career arc."

Taylor delivers the May 2022 NYU Commencement Address at Yankee Stadium, joking, "I'm 90 percent sure the reason I'm here is because I have a song called '22.'" She went on to give the audience advice about coping with adversity, based on what she learned from being canceled and getting "publicly humiliated over and over again."

Accept That No One Needs a Legitimate Reason to Hate You

"Criticism that's constructive is helpful to my character growth. Baseless criticism is stuff I've got to toss out now," Taylor shared with *Rolling Stone* in 2019. "People had so much fun hating me, and they didn't really need very many reasons to do it.…And I couldn't figure out how to learn from it. Because I wasn't sure exactly what I did that was so wrong. That was really hard for me, because I cannot stand it when people can't take criticism. So I try to self-examine, and even though that's really hard and hurts a lot sometimes, I really try to understand where people are coming from when they don't like me. And I completely get why people wouldn't like me. Because, you know, I've had my insecurities say those things—and things 1,000 times worse."

Taylor hugs one of her idols, Carole King, backstage at the 2021 Rock & Roll Hall of Fame Induction Ceremony. Taylor opened the ceremony by performing King's "Will You Still Love Me Tomorrow." In her speech honoring King, Taylor said, "Carole taught artists like me that telling your own story is worth the work and struggle it takes to earn the opportunity for your story to be heard."

Focus on What You Love

"I think there are two things that have protected me over the course of my career," Taylor told *Entertainment Tonight* in 2020. "The first thing is my enthusiasm and the second thing is how much I love music," she said. "As soon as you fail, enthusiasm tells you that the next great idea is around the corner. And your love of music will always center you if you're doing this for that and that alone, because that is hard to take away. People can reduce and criticize other elements but…it sounds really simple, but loving the actual making of music and playing music has really helped me balance things."

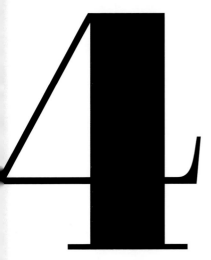

Embrace Your Enthusiasm

"There is false stigma around eagerness in our culture of unbothered ambivalence. This outlook perpetuates the idea that it's not cool to want it. That people who don't try are fundamentally more chic than those who do," Taylor said during her 2022 commencement address at NYU. "I wouldn't know, because I've been a lot of things, but I've never been an expert on 'chic'. But I'm the one who's up here [onstage] so you have to listen to me when I say this: Never be ashamed of trying. Effortlessness is a myth. The people who wanted it the least were the ones I wanted to date and be friends with in high school. The people who wanted it most are the people I now hire to work for my company."

In her 2022 song "Anti-Hero," Taylor sings, "I have this thing where I get older but just never wiser." Despite those lyrics, she has found a wise path to survive and thrive through the challenges of always being in the spotlight and always being judged. Luckily for her millions of fans, she's generous enough to share what she has learned in case it helps them too.

"All Too Well"

TAYLOR'S DIRECTORIAL DEBUT

After *Red* was released in 2012, the seething "All Too Well" became a cult favorite. Its vivid imagery and to-the-bone depiction of a fracturing relationship struck a chord with many listeners. Later, cowriter Liz Rose said that though the song was just 5 minutes, 28 seconds, the original version was "probably 10, 12, or 15 minutes long!" Her comments fueled fan speculation that the song had much more to tell than what was in its official release.

When *Red (Taylor's Version)* came out in 2021, the extended rerecording of "All Too Well" clocked in at 10 minutes, 13 seconds. The new version fleshed out the relationship between a wide-eyed young woman and a knowing older man in ways that stretched the song's tension to a near-breaking point.

Swifties were there for it, streaming it 54 million times during its first week of release. That devotion propelled the song to number one on the Hot 100 in November 2021, making it the longest song to reach the singles chart's summit.

Taylor then made her debut as a filmmaker, when she wrote and directed the video for the song. Among the many awards it garnered, the short film won Video of the Year and Best Direction at the 2022 MTV Video Music Awards, the first for a self-directed work.

In November 2021, Taylor arrives at NYC's AMC Lincoln Center in a chic velvet pantsuit for the premiere of *All Too Well: The Short Film.*

Taylor takes photos with fans at the November 2012 Aria Awards in Australia. She is famous for going out of her way to make her fans feel special.

"YOU BELONG WITH ME"

AN ODE TO SWIFTIES

After Taylor Swift attended a Kansas City Chiefs game at Arrowhead Stadium in September 2023, ticket sales soared and future Chiefs games saw Super Bowl–level viewership.

When her Eras Tour rolled into town, it significantly boosted local economies, with each fan averaging $1,300 in spending on travel, hotel, food, and merch.

When she challenged Swifties to solve 33 million puzzles to reveal the vault track title on the 2023 release of *1989 (Taylor's Version)*, they temporarily broke Google with their enthusiastic response.

Like fans at all stops on the Eras Tour, the Los Angeles tour attendees were enthusiastic. However, the 70,000 fans took it a step further at the August 5, 2023 show, dancing so wildly that they caused seismic activity equivalent to a 2.3 magnitude earthquake. Fans in Seattle did the same on July 29, 2023.

The story of Taylor's megawatt stardom and ever-upward success is often told through the lens of what her fans—Swifties like me—have done for her: the records we've helped her shatter, the haters and corporations we've condemned into apologizing, the lines we've formed, and the hours we've waited to be in the proximity of her shimmer.

And while impressive, that arc assumes one-sided devotion. Swifties will post into the void, spend money they may not have, and even skip their weddings to remind Taylor that they see her in the way we all want our partners to view us—with unending pride and devotion.

It has never mattered to us if Taylor sees her fans the same way too. She does, though.

For the nearly 20 years of her career in country and pop music, Taylor Swift has masterminded a world of abundance for her fans. There's the music, of course, and the Swiftian multiverse of ex-lovers, fictional characters, and interwoven storylines for listeners to slip into and out of as they please. There's also the fandom, where Swifties say their leader's commitment to kindness, positivity,

and reciprocity has led them to create lasting friendships. As a Swiftie, you could go anywhere in Taylor's kingdom and never feel lonely.

Then there's also the matter of Taylor herself, who has long been a fan of her fans. From the moment she joined the blogging platform Tumblr in 2014, she has practiced pastel-tinted surveillance, lurking as Swifties posted about her and laughing along with the jokes.

Sometimes, like during Swiftmas, she sends presents, homemade cookies, and handwritten letters to the people behind her favorite fan accounts. Other times, she breaks the fourth wall to clue us into the Easter eggs we love so dearly, keeping up the hunt by acknowledging her favorite fan theories with a simple Like on Tumblr, installing cryptic murals, or cheering us on as we discover hints in her music that she didn't intend to leave. (The generosity of Taylor's imagination knows no bounds, after all.)

Most often, she deputizes Taylor Nation, her official fan club, to handpick Swifties she wants to meet. These meetings can happen either backstage at her concerts or inside one of her homes for a Secret

Super-Swiftie Molly Swindall poses with part of her vast Taylor Swift vinyl collection, which she feels embodies her loyalty to the singer. "I know that I stayed by [Taylor] through every single era, through all the thick and thin," Swindall told *the Washington Post* in October 2023. "That's something that I get to be proud of—that whether it was cool or not, I was a fan."

Session, the intimate listening parties that have included conversations with her parents, snuggles with her cats, and ample one-on-one time with the star herself.

Maya Minocha was invited to be one of those Secret Sessioners. She became a fan of Taylor's as an 8-year-old in Kansas City. She remembers begging her mom to let her be late to swim practice so she could listen to "Tim McGraw" in its entirety. Minocha said Taylor "felt like she was my friend from jump," but Taylor actually became something like a friend after Taylor invited Minocha into her Rhode Island home for one of the *1989* Secret Sessions in 2014.

Minocha can still recount every sensory detail of the event a decade later, from the jokes she told that made Taylor laugh to the singer's bare feet padding around the kitchen to the

giggles of guests during the "Shake It Off" dance party Taylor initiated in her living room.

Minocha reconnected with Taylor a year later when she posted a video asking the star to hit her in the face with a golf club, like one of the cars in the "Blank Space" music video. She was invited backstage where Taylor, golf club in hand, deadpanned, "Maya, let's do this." Minocha was thrilled, saying, "I genuinely have an inside joke with Taylor Swift," along with the fact that it is now a part of Swiftie lore.

It's these personal interactions that help Taylor inhabit the liminal space between celebrity, friend, role model, and something just shy of all-knowing deity. After Taylor incorporated fan Mikael Arellano's viral "Bejeweled" TikTok dance into her Eras Tour choreography, she invited him to attend a show of his choosing as a thank-you. During the second night of the tour's stint in Philadelphia, Taylor brought Arellano to the front of the stage during "22," shook his hand, and handed him her signed prop hat. "It was surreal," Arellano said. "I wonder if she thinks about me a lot, since she does my dance every day" of her tour.

Taylor gifts her fans with spaces to retreat to, while also providing building blocks for moments they want to be present for. "The world she creates is an escape from the real world... I love getting to look forward to things that she does," said Amanda Schwerdtman, 26, who became a Swiftie in grade school while learning to play every song on the singer's self-titled debut album. She eventually met Taylor at the 2023 Los Angeles premiere of the Eras Tour concert movie, where the singer spent two hours greeting fans individually.

Taylor sometimes takes a step back to let fans create and tend to their own set of traditions, growing friendships and communities that exist both separate from Taylor and because of her. Sometimes that looks like beading bracelets to pass out during shows because of a lyric from

"You're on Your Own, Kid." Other times, it looks like helping strangers secure last-minute concert tickets or voting in elections because being a Swiftie means showing up with earnest. Because that's what Taylor has taught us to do all along.

—BEATRICE FORMAN

March 2023–December 2024

Eras *Tour*

The success of the Eras Tour, which kicked off on March 17, 2023, was by design, as Taylor laid the groundwork with 17 years of hits. But could she have known that it would be the highest-grossing music tour ever, the first to surpass $1 billion in revenue? The record-breaking tour raked in an estimated 4.35 million tickets for the first 60 shows. Both a financial and cultural juggernaut, the tour was worth the price of admission, with multiple set and costume changes and Taylor performing at the top of her game. And Swifties made it a joyful celebration, coming dressed in their favorite era and singing and dancing nonstop throughout the three-hour show.

BY THE NUMBERS

2023 ERAS TOUR

66 shows

4M fans attended

$900M grossed

Taylor wears a stunning Roberto Cavalli dress during the *Fearless* portion of the Eras Tour in Arizona in March 2023. During this set, Taylor typically plays "You Belong with Me," "Love Story," and "Fearless."

LEFT: Taylor rocks a one-legged snake-adorned Roberto Cavalli jumpsuit, a nod to Karyn, for the *reputation* set of the April 2023 Eras Tour in Tampa, Florida. A snake shape also slithered through the bracelets handed out to concertgoers at each show. **ABOVE:** Taylor and her dancers pause for a moment during the *Red* set of the Eras Tour in June 2023 in Cincinnati. The *Red* era features a special interaction between Taylor and the crowd: Each night at the end of "22," she skips to the end of the stage and gives one lucky fan her autographed custom hat designed by Los Angeles–based Gladys Tamez, like the one she's wearing here.

Taylor opens her July 2023 stop in Kansas City in one of four *Lover* bodysuits she wore during the first year of the Eras Tour. *USA Today* also noted that she wore "three *Fearless* dresses, two *evermore* dresses, six *Speak Now* gowns, three bedazzled '22' shirts, five *folkore* dresses, four *1989* crop top and skirt combos, six *Midnights* T-shirt dresses, three 'Midnight Rain' bodysuits and four 'Karma' faux fur jackets." Taylor debuted 10 new looks for the second leg of the tour, which began in Paris in May 2024.

Taylor performs "I Can Do It With a Broken Heart" in a Vivienne Westwood white crepe tailcoat with silver crystal-embellished satin lapels and a three-row pearl orb choker in May 2024 in Paris. In order to make room for *The Tortured Poets Department* songs, she combined the *folklore* and *evermore* sets and cut a few songs including "The Archer" from *Lover* and "Long Live" from *Speak Now*.

A fan shows a ticket from the VIP merch outside the stadium of FC Club River Plate, where Taylor makes her first appearance in Argentina in November 2023. A group of nearly 100 superfans rotated waiting in line for six months in order to get tickets. After the three shows quickly sold out, the waiting list grew to 2.8 million people.

"MASTERMIND"

SWIFTONOMICS

Since she burst onto the scene in 2006, Taylor's business acumen has rivaled her songwriting skills. Her first solo *Fearless* tour earned $66 million, making it the 15th highest-grossing tour of 2010. Since then, each tour has increased in revenue, and the Eras Tour is projected to earn her $2.2 billion, while also generating an estimated $5 billion for local economies. Through the success of her tours, Taylor has used her influence to partner with Ticketmaster to minimize scalping by helping create a verified-fan program.

For the Eras concert film, Taylor cut out the studio middlemen and worked directly with distributors, paving the way for other artists to retain more of their revenue. It has become the highest-grossing concert and documentary film of all time, taking in nearly $188 million during its nine-week initial run in theaters.

Since leaving Big Machine Records, Taylor has made owning her masters a linchpin of her business strategy. These rereleases have also significantly increased her streaming output in recent years. In 2023, she earned $100 million+ in streaming royalties from Spotify alone, with Billboard estimating that she earned $200 million from all streaming platforms. Her savvy marketing has also led to a resurgence in vinyl sales, with *Midnights* selling 575,000 copies on top of 549.26 million streams in its first week.

Taylor's financial impact was so significant in 2023 that the Federal Reserve cited her as a factor in third-quarter economic growth the United States. "If you fail to plan, you plan to fail, Strategy sets the scene for the tale," she sings in "Mastermind," which in this case is the story of a financial dynamo at the height of her power.

LEFT: When *The Eras Tour: The Concert Movie (Taylor's Version)* was released on Disney+ in March 2024, it featured five bonus songs, including "cardigan," which she is seen here performing in Singapore that month. It was streamed 4.6 million times in the first three days, making it the number one music film ever on the platform.
BELOW: Taylor hugs boyfriend Travis Kelce after his team's Super Bowl victory in 2024. Her support for him and the Kansas City Chiefs throughout the 2023 season was a boon for the NFL. Her appearances at games are widely thought to explain the 9 percent increase in female football viewers over the season.

"The fans are amazing. I can't believe how much they care. You have no idea how much fun it is to make stuff for people who care about it that much."

—TAYLOR, *GOOD MORNING AMERICA,* April 2019

Wearing a stunning Elie Saab dress, Taylor looks over her shoulder during the second of three nights in her hometown of Nashville, from May 5 to 7, 2024. The next night, storms caused a delay in the show start time. She ended up taking the stage at 10:00 pm, only to get drenched, telling the crowd, "This is something we're all doing together. It's like such a bonding experience. We're all gonna leave here tonight looking like we just went through five car washes....People will be like, 'Where were you? Several wars?' And you're like, 'No, I just went to the Eras Tour. It's fine.'"

Jacqueline Deval VP, Publisher
Zach Mattheus Group Creative Director
Nicole Fisher Deputy Director
Maria Ramroop Deputy Managing Editor
Caroline Pickering Cover Designer
Estee Brooke Friedman Deputy Copy Chief

INDELIBLE EDITIONS

Produced by INDELIBLE EDITIONS
Dinah Dunn Editorial Director
Andrea Duarte Creative Director
Nanette Bendyna-Schuman Copyeditor
Susan Lee Proofreader

Library of Congress Cataloging-in-Publication
Data Available on request

10 9 8 7 6 5 4 3 2 1

Published by Hearst Home, an imprint of
Hearst Books/Hearst Magazine Media, Inc.
300 W 57th Street
New York, NY 10019

Printed in Canada
978-1-958395-68-4

Ranking the 50 best Taylor Swift songs is *hard*,
but someone's gotta do it. Scan the QR code to
see how the Swifties at *Cosmopolitan* take on
the task. Plus, you'll find more up-to-the-minute
Taylor Swift news at **cosmopolitan.com**.

PHOTO CREDITS Collin Peterson: 58, 62; **George Holz:** 38, 43; **Getty Images:** ACMA2020/Getty Images for ACM: 108-109; Allen J. Schaben / Los Angeles Times via Getty Images: 125; Amy Sussman: 106; ANGELA WEISS/AFP: 116; Ashok Kumar/TAS24/ Getty Images for TAS Rights Management: 140; Bruce Glikas/FilmMagic: 110; Bryan Bedder/Getty Images for AEG: 114; Buda Mendes/TAS23/Getty Images for TAS Rights Management: 18; Chris Polk/FilmMagic: 60; Christopher Polk/MTV1415/Getty Images for MTV: 93; Christopher Polk/NBC/NBCU Photo Bank: 113; Christopher Polk /TAS/Getty Images for TAS: 4, 20, 26, 68-69; Dave Hogan/ABA: 105; David Livingston: 63; Dimitrios Kambouris: 96, 120; Dimitrios Kambouris/ LP5/Getty Images for TAS: 12; Don Arnold/TAS18/ Getty Images: 100-101; Don Arnold/WireImage: 122; Emma McIntyre/TAS23/Getty Images for TAS Rights Management: 4; Ethan Miller: 23, 48, 102-103; Ezra Shaw: 141; Fernando Gens/picture alliance via Getty Image: 138; Gotham/GC Images: 104; Jamie McCarthy/FilmMagic: 98; Jason Kempin/Getty Images for Erickson Public Relations: 52, 53; Jason Merritt: 65; Jeff Kravitz/FilmMagic: 75, 76; Jeff Kravitz/TAS23/ Getty Images for TAS Rights Management: 32-33; Jesse D. Garrabrant/NBAE via Getty Images: 13; John Leyba/The Denver Post via Getty Images: 15; John Shearer/Getty Images for TAS Rights Management: 3, 22, 134-135, 142-143; John Shearer/WireImage: 46-47, 55-56, 66-67, 72-73; Karwai Tang/WireImage: 99; Keith Bedford/Starbucks: 74; Kendrick Brinson for The Washington Post via Getty Images: 126-127; Kevin Kane/Getty Images for Jingle Ball 2012: 81; Kevin Mazur: 84; Kevin Mazur/Getty Images for The Recording Academy: 24, 112; Kevin Mazur/Getty Images for The Rock and Roll Hall of Fame: 118; Kevin Mazur/TAS/ Getty Images for TAS Rights Management: 2, 6, 8-9, 31, 34, 130-131, 136-137; Kevin Mazur/ WireImage: 42, 78-79, 87, 88, 98; Kevin Winter: 80; Kevin Winter/ACMA/Getty Images for ACMA: 49; Kevin Winter/Getty Images for TAS Rights Management: 16-17, 21; Kevork Djansezian: 54; Larry Busacca: 77, 97, 99; Larry Busacca/Getty Images for Country Music Hall of Fame: 76; Larry Busacca/Getty Images for Erickson Public Relations: 10; Michael Buckner/ ACMA/Getty Images for ACMA: 41; Octavio Jones/ TAS23/Getty Images for for TAS Rights Management: 132; Rick Diamond: 128; Rick Diamond/Wireimage: 2, 14, 50, 64; Scott Gries: 45; Stephen Lovekin: 96, 97; Steve Granitz/WireImage: 94, 129; TAS Rights Management 2021 via Getty Images: 111; Taylor Hill/ TAS23/Getty Images for TAS Rights Management: 133; Terence Rushin/TAS23/Getty Images for TAS Rights Management: 144; Theo Wargo/WireImage for Clear Channel Radio New York: 19; Tristan Fewings/Getty Images for Swarovski: 91; Vince Bucci/Getty Images for AMA: 51; **Matt Jones:** cover, back cover, 1, 3-4, 70, 82

**Taylor throws her signature
move, a hand heart, at the April
2023 Eras Tour stop in Atlanta.**